ADDITIONAL MEDIA LABS & WEB INVESTIGATIONS

PEGGY BRICKMAN
UNIVERSITY OF GEORGIA

ISOBEL HEATHCOTE
UNIVERSITY OF GUELPH

BIOLOGY
A GUIDE TO THE NATURAL WORLD

David Krogh

Prentice Hall
Upper Saddle River, NJ 07458

Editor in Chief, Biology: *Sheri Snavely*
Project Manager: *Karen Horton*
Special Projects Manager: *Barbara A. Murray*
Cover Designer: *Joseph Sengotta*
Manufacturing Manager: *Trudy Pisciotti*
Copyeditor/Interior Designer: *Chris Thillen*

© 2001 by Prentice Hall
Upper Saddle River, NJ 07458

All rights reserved. No part of this book may
be reproduced, in any form or by any means,
without permission in writing from the publisher.

Printed in the United States of America

10 9 8 7 6 5 4 3 2 1

0-13-092083-5

Prentice-Hall International (UK) Limited, *London*
Prentice-Hall of Australia Pty. Limited, *Sydney*
Prentice-Hall Canada Inc., *Toronto*
Prentice-Hall Hispanoamericana, S.A., *Mexico*
Prentice-Hall of India Private Limited, *New Delhi*
Pearson Education of Asia, Pte., Ltd., *Singapore*
Prentice-Hall of Japan, Inc., *Tokyo*
Editoria Prentice -Hall do Brasil, Ltda., *Rio de Janeiro*

Contents

Part 1: MediaLabs

Would We Miss Them If They Were Gone? Organelles   8

Do We Know Too Much? Human Genetic Testing   10

Can We Stop the Cycle? DNA to RNA to Protein   12

El Niño and the Breadbasket: How Climate Affects Our Weather, Food, and Water Supplies   14

Part 2: Web Investigations

Genetics
Critiquing Information   18
Mitochondria   18
Cell Cycle   18
Mitosis   18
Y Chromosome   19
Meiosis   19
Dihybrid Crosses   19
Twins   19
Mendelian Traits   20
Epistasis   20
Genetic Counseling   20
Alcoholism   20
Translation   21
Information   21
Lactose Operon   21
Polymerase Chain Reaction (PCR)   21
DNA Testing   22
Phylogeny   22

Anatomy and Physiology
pH   22
Basal Metabolic Rate (BMR)   22
Connective Tissue   23
Bone Density   23
Bone Quizzes   23
Knee Structure   23
Spinal Cord Injury   23
Brain Probe   24
Allergies   24
Heart Murmurs   24
GI Tract Quiz   24
Dehydration   24

Part 2: Web Investigations (cont.)

    Impotence   25
    Reproduction Quiz   25
    Human Development Time Line   25
    Surfactant Production   25

Ecology and Environmental Science
    Biodiversity   26
    Biogeochemical Cycles as a Tool for Environmental Management   27
    Biotechnology in Agriculture: Weighing Risks against Benefits   28
    Certifiably Sustainable?   29
    The Ecology of Estuarine Ecosystems   29
    Fire in Protected Ecosystems: Friend or Foe?   30
    Managing Water Resources on a Watershed Basis   31
    Measuring Species Change   32
    Pests: Kill 'Em or Eat 'Em?   33
    Tracking Demographic Change   34

Cross-reference to Chapters in *Biology: A Guide to the Natural World*.

Part 1: MediaLabs

Would We Miss Them If They Were Gone? Organelles	Chapter 4
Do We Know Too Much? Human Genetic Testing	Chapter 12
Can We Stop the Cycle? DNA to RNA to Protein	Chapter 14
El Niño and the Breakbasket: How Climate Affects Our Weather, Food, and Water Supplies	Chapter 29

Part 2: Web Investigations

Genetics

Critiquing Information	Chapter 1, pp. 8–9
Mitochondria	Chapter 4, p. 81
Cell Cycle	Chapter 9, pp. 188–189
Mitosis	Chapter 9, pp. 188–189
Y Chromosome	Chapter 10, p. 198
Meiosis	Chapter 10, pp. 204–205
Dihybrid Crosses	Chapter 11, p. 218
Twins	Chapter 11, p. 223
Mendelian Traits	Chapter 11, pp. 226–227
Epistasis	Chapter 12, pp. 238–239
Genetic Counseling	Chapter 12, pp. 242–243
Alcoholism	Chapter 12, p. 247
Translation	Chapter 14, pp. 272–275
Information	Chapter 14
Lactose Operon	Chapter 14, pp. 278–279
Polymerase Chain Reaction (PCR)	Chapter 15, p. 291
DNA Testing	Chapter 15, pp. 294–295
Phylogeny	Chapter 18, pp. 361–362

Anatomy and Physiology

pH	Chapter 3, pp. 40–43
Basal Metabolic Rate (BMR)	Chapter 7, pp. 142–143
Connective Tissue	Chapter 23, pp. 485–489
Bone Density	Chapter 23, p. 496
Bone Quizzes	Chapter 23, p. 497
Knee Structure	Chapter 23, p. 498
Spinal Cord Injury	Chapter 24, pp. 512–513
Brain Probe	Chapter 24, p. 514
Allergies	Chapter 24, pp. 531–532
Heart Murmurs	Chapter 25, p. 546
GI Tract Quiz	Chapter 25, p. 558
Dehydration	Chapter 25, pp. 562–563
Impotence	Chapter 27, p. 596
Reproduction Quiz	Chapter 27, p. 597

Part 2: Web Investigations (cont.)

Human Development Time Line	Chapter 27, p. 601
Surfactant Production	Chapter 27, p. 602

Ecology and Environmental Science

Biodiversity	Chapter 20, pp. 392–416; Chapter 21, pp. 478–479; Chapter 28, pp. 625–636
Biogeochemical Cycles as a Tool for Environmental Management	Chapter 3, pp. 43–47; Chapter 21, pp. 424–425; Chapter 29, pp. 646–651
Biotechnology in Agriculture: Weighing Risks against Benefits	Chapter 15, pp. 286–293 and 297–299
Certifiably Sustainable?	Chapter 22, pp. 457–460; Chapter 28, pp. 635–636 and 663–667
The Ecology of Estuarine Ecosystems	Chapter 28, pp. 614 and 644–677
Fire in Protected Ecosystems: Friend or Foe?	Chapter 22, pp. 457–460; Chapter 28, pp. 635–636 and 663–667
Managing Water Resources on a Watershed Basis	Chapter 29, pp. 649–651, 659–662, and 670–671
Measuring Species Change	Unit 3 (Chapters 9–15); Chapter 17, p. 329; Chapter 28, pp. 626–627
Pests: Kill 'Em or Eat 'Em?	Chapter 20, pp. 392–416; Chapter 21, pp. 478–479; Chapter 28, pp. 625–636
Tracking Demographic Change	Chapter 28, pp. 614–624

Part 1: MediaLabs

MediaLab
Would We Miss Them If They Were Gone? Organelles

Catastrophic damage to your liver, lung, heart, or even kidneys can lead to complete organ failure. Under these circumstances, the only cure is finding a new, healthy organ to replace the old one. An organ is irreplaceable because each performs a unique function for our bodies. Similarly, each organelle performs a unique function within our cells and cannot substitute for another kind of organelle if it is damaged or defective. Most of us are familiar with the consequence of organ failure, but can you imagine what might occur in organelle failure? In the *CD Activity*, you'll review some of the functions performed by organelles, and in the *Web Investigation* you can read about new studies linking many genetic illnesses and some of the decline seen with aging to malfunctioning organelles.

Text relating to this *MediaLab* can be found in Chapter 4 of your textbook; the animations are on your CD-ROM.

CD ACTIVITY

Eukaryotic cells sequester cellular activities in discrete (often membrane-enclosed) structures within their cytoplasm, called organelles. This *CD Activity* will lead you through two of the important activities performed by organelles, the manufacture of proteins, and the digestion of defective organelles.

Activity

1. *There are tens of thousands of different proteins inside a cell. They perform the lion's share of cellular functions and must be located in the specific organelle where they are needed. This series of animations leads you through the protein production pathway.* (See the animation of Figure 4.5, "Path of Protein Production in the Cell," on your CD-ROM. You will find it in the Chapter 4 animation library.)

2. *All organelles break down over time and must be removed and recycled. You will then view an animation of this process.* (See the animation of Figure 4.9, "Cellular Recycling." On your CD-ROM. You will find it in the Chapter 4 animation library.)

Now that you have reviewed how proteins are processed and organelles recycled by lysosomes, in the following section you can investigate some medical consequences of interfering with these activities.

WEB INVESTIGATION

Investigation 1
Estimated time for completion = 5 minutes

You know that lysosomes digest food and defective organelles, but did you know our cells also use lysosomes to dispose of harmful bacteria? Go to the following website to view an animation of what happens inside a cell fighting off a salmonella bacterium, a common cause of food poisoning.

http://www.hhmi.org/biointeractive/animations.html

Investigation 2
Estimated time for completion = 5 minutes

Just how important are lysosomes to our cells? Well, at least 30 different human genetic diseases, many lethal, are caused by a defect in production of lysosomal enzymes. These defective enzymes often accumulate inside the cell, as well as in the bloodstream and urine, and commonly result in developmental defects, defects in the neural and immune systems, skeletal abnormalities, and death at an early age. Go to:

http://mcrcr2.med.nyu.edu/murphp01/lysosome/dischart.htm

Select one of the lysosomal storage disorders. Read as much information as you can about the disorder. What is the exact problem with the lysosomes? What symptoms are observed? Is there a genetic test available for the disease? Have they identified the gene responsible, and will this lead to a treatment?

Investigation 3
Estimated time for completion = 10 minutes

Plaques in our arteries and brains, osteoporosis, sagging skin, age spots— all these are symptoms of aging. Why do they occur? One of the hot theories explaining why our tissues age is accumulated cellular damage. One sign of damage is the brown pigment called lipofuscin, "the aging pigment," that accumulates in older cells, especially liver and heart. The pigment results from oxidative degradation of mitochondria and/or lysosomes. You say you don't want to have liver spots? Hasn't somebody come up with a cure? Many are trying. To read an article from the Life Extension Foundation go to:

http://www.lef.org/magazine/mag99/sept99_report2.html

COMMUNICATE YOUR RESULTS

Exercise 1
Estimated time for completion = 5 minutes

The salmonella bacterium actually plays right into the hands of its host cell during invasion by actually causing itself to be engulfed into a vacuole destined for destruction in the lysosome. What goes wrong? In 20 words, can you describe why the lysosome does not digest the bacterium inside the food vacuole?

Exercise 2
Estimated time for completion = 5 minutes

Prepare a 50 word description of the lysosomal storage disorder you investigated in web investigation 2 to inform your classmates about these devastating diseases.

Exercise 3
Estimated time for completion = 5 minutes

Freeze your head? Exercise more? Vitamins? You want to live a long full life, but according to the article you read in the web investigation 3, what is currently the only demonstrated mechanism for extending maximum lifespan? Why should this work? Compose a 50-word description of one of the observed physical changes resulting from eating less and explain why this should help you live longer.

MediaLab
Do We Know Too Much? Human Genetic Testing

Collum is an 8-month-old baby with an incurable neurodegenerative disorder. In a few short weeks he changes from a playful, robust infant to being unable to lift his head, to move, and eventually even to breathe. When reading heartbreaking accounts about battling these kinds of rare conditions, you may ask why it happens, what medical science is doing for a cure, and if it can happen to your child. Doctors have recently discovered the cause of many of these illnesses; unfortunately, they are genetic mutations passed from parent to child during conception. Today there are few treatment options for repairing mutations. With this discouraging news, the only solace may be that we can now predict the chance of a future child or grandchild suffering the same fate. Given what you know about human genetics from reading Chapter 12, can you to predict your child's chance of inheriting some disorder? In the following *CD Activity*, you review the three patterns of inheritance of genetic mutations, so that in the *Web Investigation* you can analyze your skills as a human geneticist.

Text relating to this *MediaLab* can be found in Chapter 12 of your textbook.

CD ACTIVITY

Human genetics uses Mendel's rules about the probability of inheriting a specific genetic characteristic and extends them to predicting inheritance of human diseases. This *CD Activity* will lead you through the three main patterns of inheritance seen in human genetics.

Activity

1. *First, you will see how to create a Punnett Square to predict the chance of a child inheriting a recessive condition caused by a mutation on one of human chromosomes 1–22, called autosomes.* (See the animation of Figure 12.4a, "Autosomal Recessive Inheritance," in the Chapter 12 animation library CD-ROM.)

2. *Next, you can compare that with the probability of inheriting a condition caused by a dominant mutation on one of the autosomes.* (See the animation of Figure 12.4b, "Autosomal Dominant Inheritance" in the Chapter 12 animation library on your CD-ROM.)

3. *Finally, you can see the special inheritance pattern seen for mutations on the X chromosome, by using the example of white eyes in* Drosophila. (See the animation of Figure 12.3s, "Why All Morgan's White-Eyed F2s Were Males" in Chapter 12 animation library on your CD-ROM.)

WEB INVESTIGATION

Investigation 1
Estimated time for completion = 10 minutes

Genetic counselors are health professionals who specialize in disseminating information on over 4,000 different inherited human diseases. They take detailed family histories, review basic genetics, and counsel patients on the likelihood of inheriting one of thousands of disorders, while dealing with the emotional and sometimes moral issues involved. How do you know if you should see a genetic counselor? Would you understand the basic genetics they explained to you? For an article describing gene testing, go to:

http://www.accessexcellence.org/AE/AEPC/NIH/index.html

Investigation 2
Estimated time for completion = 5 minutes

In the future portrayed in the 1997 movie *Gattaca*, prenatal genetic screening helps couples chose the perfect child, free from mutations that would predispose heart disease, low IQ, or even myopia. To visit the future and try your hand at designing your offspring, go to:

>http://www.spe.sony.com/Pictures/SonyMovies/movies/Gattaca/design_child.htm

What would you select for your child's height, weight, health problems, and even IQ if you could?

Investigation 3
Estimated time for completion = 5 minutes

How close is science getting to science fiction? In *Web Investigation 2*, you tried to design the perfect child. How many of the traits like Alzheimer's, drug addiction, arthritis, even height that you listed as undesirable in your family can now be tested for? Visit the following website:

>http://www.geneclinics.org/profiles/disclaimer-index.html

When you get there, click on <u>View all Diseases</u> to investigate one of the hundreds of genetic mutations for which tests are currently available. Pick one of the genetic diseases that runs in your family, and investigate the state of research into treatments and predictive gene testing.

COMMUNICATE YOUR RESULTS

Exercise 1
Estimated time for completion = 15 minutes

If someone could test your DNA and tell you what diseases you would likely suffer from in 25 years, would you want to know the results? Using the article from *Web Investigation 1*, compose a 250-word paper supporting or refuting your personal decision to know the results of your own gene test. Use examples, including the specific disease you would be tested for, the actual likelihood of contracting the disease if you have a positive test, how this knowledge could help you avoid dying from the disease, and how you think having this knowledge would affect you and your family.

Exercise 2
Estimated time for completion = 5 minutes

Is it even possible to design the perfect child using your genetic background? If there are undesirable traits in your family, you may need to add beneficial genes from outside your gene pool. The checklist from the *Gattaca* website uses questions similar to those a genetics counselor might ask you about your family health history. List all the "undesirable" inherited traits that run in your family.

Exercise 3
Estimated time for completion = 5 minutes

In *Web Investigation 3* you looked at one of the hundreds of human diseases with a genetic component, such as familial breast cancer, that may run in your family and can currently be tested for. Prepare a 250-word report for your own family members about the current state of knowledge on that disease and the tests available. Describe the disease and indicate how much of the severity of symptoms is due to environmental influences like diet, and how much to genetic mutations. If a DNA test is available, indicate whether you would like to know the results of the test and if the test can accurately predict who will get the disease.

MediaLab
Can We Stop the Cycle? DNA to RNA to Protein

We take for granted our control over bacteria and viruses, confident that we can stop them dead with a simple antibiotic or antiviral medication. But did you know that these medications work to control the same critical steps of transcription, translation, and protein manufacture that occur in our cells? In the *CD Activity* of this *MediaLab*, you'll review the cellular activities needed to manufacture proteins, so that in the *Web Investigation* you can analyze the subtle differences between our cells and their invaders. These differences can be exploited in our fight against the enemies within us, as you'll see in the *Communicate Your Results* section.

Text and figures relating to this *MediaLab* can be found in Chapter 14 of your textbook; the animations can be found in the Chapter 14 animation library on your CD-ROM.

CD ACTIVITY

Every one of the thousands of different proteins made by a cell is created in the same way, and the steps are similar in all cells. This *CD Activity* leads you step by step through the protein production pathway.

Activity

1. *First, you will review the two major stages in protein synthesis: (a) copying the information of DNA into RNA so that it can exit the nucleus, and (b) the actual manufacture of protein on ribosomes in the cytoplasm.* (See the animation of Figure 14.2, "Two Major Stages of Protein Production," in the animation library on your CD-ROM.)

2. *Next, you can watch a ribosome at work, and view all the other ingredients needed to translate the RNA message into protein.* (See the animation of Figure 14.10, "Translation," in the animation library on your CD-ROM.)

3. *Then, observe how ribosomes speed up production.* (See the animation of Figure 14.11, "Mass Production" in the animation library on your CD-ROM.)

4. *Finally, view one example of how production can be regulated at the level of transcription in the lac operon.* (See the animation of Figure 14.12, "Genetic Regulation in Action," on your CD-ROM.)

Now that you have reviewed the steps in protein synthesis, in the following section, you can investigate how blocking these critical steps can cripple an organism, and in the process save our lives.

WEB INVESTIGATION

Investigation 1
Estimated time for completion = 5 minutes

If you still think that the steps in making a protein are confusing, maybe you would like to try a step-by-step interactive demonstration. The following website allows you to take part in coordinating the manufacture of proteins:

http://www.pbs.org/wgbh/aso/tryit/dna/

Click on <u>DNA workshop activity</u> once you reach the site, and try your hand at using DNA in replication and in protein synthesis.

Investigation 2
Estimated time for completion = 5 minutes

You just saw two uses for DNA, replication and transcription. DNA to RNA to protein is called the central dogma, because all cells use the same steps in protein synthesis. HIV, the virus that causes AIDS, is a retrovirus, meaning it carries its genetic material as RNA, not DNA. To view the step-by-step overview of HIV infection, visit this site:

http://www.cellsalive.com/hiv0.htm

How can HIV replicate its genetic information or transcribe RNA without DNA?

Investigation 3
Estimated time for completion = 15 minutes

By now you understand how all proteins are made, but what would happen if you stopped protein synthesis? Death? Yes, but a death you can rejoice in— the death of your enemies. Enemies in this case include opportunistic bacteria that can invade your tissues and cause disease or death. Many antibiotics work by stopping transcription or translation of proteins. Read about bacteria and antibiotics by going to the following website, where you'll discover how a wide range of antibiotics act to defeat bacteria:

http://www.hhmi.org/grants/lectures/biointeractive/Antibiotics_Attack/frameset.html

COMMUNICATE YOUR RESULTS

Exercise 1
Estimated time for completion = 5 minutes

Make a table of the similarities and differences between replication and protein synthesis that you observed in the first *Web Investigation*. Include the following: When are the two processes performed? What process occurs in both? Where? What enzymes are involved? What is the result in both cases?

Exercise 2
Estimated time for completion = 5 minutes

HIV uses a special viral enzyme called *reverse transcriptase* as a critical part of its life cycle. The popular anti-HIV drug AZT works by preventing reverse transcriptase functioning. Describe what would happen to a cell that was infected with HIV when AZT is used. AZT is a thymine analog (look-alike); the only difference is that it has an N-atom on the important carbon in the ribose sugar that is needed to make covalent bonds between nucleotides. Why would this affect reverse transcription?

Exercise 3
Estimated time for completion = 15 minutes

You think your fever and sore throat are from a streptococcal infection (strep throat). Your friend offers you penicillin left over from his last bacterial infection. Would it even work on your sore throat if you really had an infection of streptococcus? How does penicillin work to kill bacterial cells, but not harm your cells? If you found out your infection was more serious (pneumonia), and the culprit was *Mycoplasma pneumoniae*, would the penicillin be effective? You decide to try a wide-spectrum antibiotic that kills many species of bacteria by preventing translation or transcription. What would your pharmacist and doctor recommend to block transcription, or translation by binding and inactivating ribosomes? Why doesn't this hurt your own translation and transcription?

MediaLab
El Niño and the Breadbasket: How Climate Affects Our Weather, Food, and Water Supplies

It's almost impossible for us to imagine what the world will be like 50 or 100 years from now. Yet that is exactly the challenge facing government agencies and scientists who are planning for world food and water supply in the next century. Will Earth's biomes, and our food and water supply, change with forces such as global warming and climatic fluctuation over the next hundred years? To answer this question, you'll examine the forces that shape climate from year to year and from decade to decade, using that information to develop projections of future conditions.

Text and art relating to this *MediaLab* can be found in Chapter 29 of your textbook; the animations can be found in the Chapter 29 animation library on your CD-ROM.

CD ACTIVITY

This *CD Activity* reviews concepts about the physical conditions that influence Earth's weather and climate, and explores their impact on the abundance of life.

Activity

1. *First, you will investigate how the relationship between the Sun and Earth cause seasonal change.*
2. *Next, you will look at how air circulation patterns influence precipitation patterns around the globe.*
3. *Finally, you will examine the implications of geographic and geologic landforms and how they influence climate and weather.*

CD 1: In the tropics, seasonal change is minor but at high latitude, closer to the north and south poles, this change can be dramatic. What causes this seasonal change and why is it different at different latitudes? To investigate these phenomena, go to the animation library in Chapter 29 on your CD-ROM and load the animation of figure 29.19 titled "Earth's Tilt and the Seasons." Notice that in the Northern Hemisphere, Earth's axis points towards the sun at some times of the year and away at others. Write a short paragraph to explain how this relationship causes the seasons. For each of the four phases illustrated in the animation, predict what season inhabitants of the Southern Hemisphere will enjoy.

CD 2: From the first CD-Activity, you discovered that the angle of the sun relative to the axis of rotation of the Earth influences the seasons. This physical relationship has other dramatic consequences. Where the sun's rays are concentrated, the tropics, it is hot and where they are spread out, the poles, it is cold. This phenomenon has a dramatic influence over the Earth's precipitation patterns. To investigate this further, load the animation of figure 29.20 titled "Earth's Atmospheric Circulation Cells." Consider that heated air rises and cooled air falls. Further, remember that rising air will drop moisture while falling air will pickup moisture. Play the animation and predict how the air circulation patterns will cause variations in precipitation and climate across the Earth. As the seasons change, how do these precipitation patterns change? Compare your predictions against figure 29.21 on page 660 of your textbook. What accounts for the differences between your idealized model and the real pattern?

Circulation patterns of the Earth's oceans also have a major influence of the global climatic patterns. The ocean's circulation patterns in combination with the climatic influences described in these CD-Activities plays a significant role in the unique weather and climatic patterns evidenced across the globe. With this foundation, you will investigate how El Niño, an irregular, long-term climatic patterns, influences life on Earth.

WEB INVESTIGATION

Investigation 1
Estimated time for completion = 15 minutes

What is El Niño, and how does it affect our climate? To begin your investigation, go to this website:

http://www.pmel.noaa.gov/toga-tao/el-nino-report.html

Read about the history and influence of the El Niño Southern Oscillation (ENSO). Describe the warm and cold extremes of this phenomenon. How frequently does the warm phase of ENSO occur, and how does it affect different parts of the world? Visit the following website:

http://www.fao.org/WAICENT/faoinfo/economic/giews/english/fs/fstoc.htm

Once there, you can view United Nations Food and Agriculture Organization maps of current and past years' unfavorable crop prospects and food supply shortfalls in different parts of the world. How might global food supply problems be helped or worsened by ENSO phenomena?

Investigation 2
Estimated time for completion = 15 minutes

Why have El Niño events become more frequent in recent decades? The answer may lie in natural long-term climatic forces that create a "conveyor belt" of ocean water circulation that lasts for many years. To read an article from Oregon State University on this process, visit this website:

http://www.sciencedaily.com/releases/1999/09/990916075409.htm

Do the phenomena described in the article represent a permanent global shift or a cyclic phenomenon? What is thought to cause the conveyor belt of ocean circulation? Is it linked to, or separate from, global warming effects?

COMMUNICATE YOUR RESULTS

Exercise 1
Estimated time for completion = 15 minutes

Using the information you have gleaned about the global effects of the ENSO phenomenon, suggest some ways that an understanding of ENSO can be used to protect global food and water supplies from year to year or over longer time periods.

Exercise 2
Estimated time for completion = 15 minutes

Which of the phenomena described in the *Web Investigations* are short term? Which are reversible? Write a 250-word summary of the relative effects of ENSO, oceanic circulation, and global warming on Earth's climate. In your view, what would constitute a worst-case combination of these phenomena? What would be a best-case combination? Can you suggest a different perspective, perhaps from a different part of the world or culture?

Part 2: Web Investigations

GENETICS

Critiquing Information
Estimated time for completion = 5 minutes

Should you believe everything that you read, see, or hear? At this point, you should be aware that fiction and misinformation are often disguised as truth; therefore, a healthy dose of skepticism is a good thing to have. Being wary of possible misinformation is only half the battle. Skills to critique what you read, see, and hear will prove valuable, especially in using the Internet. To learn more about techniques for critiquing information, visit this website:

http://www.library.ucla.edu/libraries/college/instruct/web/critical.htm

Mitochondria
Estimated time for completion = 10 minutes

Where did the organelles in eukaryotic cells come from? Dr. Lynn Margulis's endosymbiotic theory of organelle inheritance explains why organelles, such as chloroplasts and mitochondria, are maternally inherited and have their own DNA. Read this article about the origin of these organelles and think about the genetic consequences of this extraordinary event. Hypothesize about the genetic changes implied by Dr. Jeon's discovery of symbiosis between amoeba and intracellular bacteria. Where are the genes for mitochondria? Why are mitochondria maternally inherited? To complete this exercise, go to:

http://dekalb.dc.peachnet.edu/~pgore/students/w96/joshbond/symb.htm

Cell Cycle
Estimated time for completion = 10 minutes

What is the relative timing of events in the cell cycle? In this exercise, you will examine micrographs of onion cells during interphase and mitosis and empirically determine the proportion of time these cells spend in each phase of mitosis. Once you reach The Biology Project's tutorial on the cell cycle, follow the instructions and then answer these questions. What part of the cell cycle takes the most time? What are the events during that phase that take so much time? Radiation tends to damage cells undergoing mitosis to a greater degree than cells in interphase; what does this tell you about the use of radiation in treating cancer? (See Chapter 23 for information on cancer and genetics.) To complete this exercise, visit the following website:

http://www.biology.arizona.edu/cell_bio/activities/cell_cycle/cell_cycle.html

Mitosis
Estimated time for completion = 10 minutes

What are some key differences between cellular events in mitosis and meiosis? Both processes begin in interphase, but the end products are quite different. Mitosis produces a pair of genetically identical cells, whereas meiosis produces four genetically different cells. You will use micrographs of the two processes to answer the following questions. At what stage in each process do the centromeres joining the sister chromatids separate? In meiosis, at what stage do the cells become haploid? What structures are involved in moving the chromosomes to the poles in mitosis? Are the same structures acting in meiosis? In Down syndrome, one extra copy of chromosome 21 is present in all the cells of the afflicted individual. Do you think the extra copy was added in mitosis or meiosis? At what stage was it added? Where did the extra copy come from? To complete this exercise, visit this website:

http://www.iacr.bbsrc.ac.uk/notebook/courses/guide/mitosis.htm

Y Chromosome
Estimated time for completion = 15 minutes

Why is the Y chromosome so small? In many cases of genetic sex determination, females are XX and males are XY. As you know from our discussion of sex linkage in Chapter 4, the X chromosome carries a number of loci; however, the Y carries only a few loci in humans. The difference in size has important consequences for genetics, as explored in the linked website article by Ken Miller. Read the article and then think about the following questions. In humans, is the Y chromosome necessary for male development? Why are errors on the X chromosome repaired through sexual production but errors on the Y are not? How does this relate to the size of the chromosomes? Bill Rice set up an experiment in which specific autosomes were not allowed to recombine. Did his results support the idea that mistakes accumulating on the Y might be responsible for its reduction in size? To complete this exercise, visit the following website:

http://biomed.brown.edu/Faculty/M/Miller/Discover/Y.html

Meiosis
Estimated time for completion = 10 minutes

How does meiosis generate genetic variation among the gametes? Two processes occur during meiosis that generate this variation. After reading through the short tutorial on recombination during meiosis, identify the two sources of variation. Which of the processes generates variation among the four copies of a given chromosome? What would happen at the level of the genes if the homologs where not perfectly aligned during crossing over, so that unequal parts of the chromosomes were exchanged? Which process accounts for Mendel's postulates of segregation and independent assortment (Chapter 3)? To complete this exercise, visit this website:

http://www.iacr.bbsrc.ac.uk/notebook/courses/guide/mitosis.htm

Dihybrid Crosses
Estimated time for completion = 15 minutes

Now that you have practiced formulating hypotheses and tests for single traits, let's try a dihybrid cross. Wild-type *Drosophila melanogaster* have oval eyes and brown bodies. Suppose you are given a fly with *lobe* eyes and an *ebony* body. Assume that these traits are not sex-linked (Chapter 4) and are on separate chromosomes (Chapter 5). You should read the introduction to using Virtual Fly Lab once you enter the linked website. Set up a cross with a wild-type female and a *lobe-eyed, ebony-bodied* male. Would it matter if one fly were *lobe-eyed* and one were *ebony-bodied*? Write down your hypotheses regarding the dominance and recessiveness of these two traits and derive a set of predictions using Punnett squares. Make the cross and observe the phenotype of the F_1. Does this provide enough information to test your predictions, or do you need to cross the F_1 and observe the F_2? If you think you have enough information, elect to test your hypothesis and enter your predictions in the box, ignoring the information regarding sex. Does the X^2 test allow you to reject your hypothesis or not? To complete this exercise, visit the following website:

http://www.blc.arizona.edu/courses/181gh/rick/genetics2/default.html

Twins
Estimated time for completion = 10 minutes

How can we study quantitative genetic traits in humans? With experimental organisms, we can set up families and breeding experiments to estimate the genetic influences on quantitative traits, but it would be unethical to perform experiments of this sort on people. Many researchers studying physical and mental disease, personality traits, and estimates of intelligence use data on monozygotic (MZ) and dizygotic (DZ) twins to infer what portion of such traits might have a genetic basis. Read the summary of twin research on left-handedness. Why does the similarity in concordance of handedness in MZ and DZ twins imply an environmental influence? The summary suggests a possible genetic effect ton handedness due to correlations between handedness in mothers and both sons and daughters, and between handedness in fathers and sons. Can you think of an environmental explanation for these correlations? To complete this exercise, visit the following website:

http://www.ben2.ucla.edu/~rjabdel/twin.html

Mendelian Traits
Estimated time for completion = 10 minutes

In this exercise, you will practice making predictions about the genetic basis of flower color in peas, one of the traits studied by Mendel. Peas have either white or purple flowers. Mendel postulated that some factor present in the gametes affected flower color. He was confident that when the sperm and the ova united, two copies of the white gamete would make a white flower and two copies of the purple gamete would make a purple flower; but what if the zygote received one white and one purple? Clearly such flowers were either white or purple, not intermediate, so one factor must be dominant over the other one. Read about dominance in Chapter 3. How would you set up a test to see if the white factor was dominant over purple, or vice versa? State your hypothesis regarding dominance and outline the predictions you would make if a true-breeding white stock were crossed with a true-breeding purple stock. What genotype(s) would be present in each stock? What would be the genotype of their progeny? Interpret the results of the crosses. Which hypothesis was supported? To complete this exercise, visit the following website:

http://www.sonic.net/~nbs/projects/anthro201/disc/

Epistasis
Estimated time for completion = 10 minutes

Epistasis occurs when the genotype at one locus modifies the phenotypic expression of another locus. Epistasis effects are very common among the genes affecting mammalian fur color. You will examine a table of loci that influence the coloration of horses and search for cases of epistatic interaction. In horses, the main gene affecting color is the E locus. The black allele (E) is dominant of the red allele (e). One example of epistasis is the A locus; if a horse is black, then the presence of the dominant A allele will restrict the black coloring to the "points" (i.e., the legs, nose, ears, and tail), whereas a recessive homozygote will be black all over. Suppose you encounter an all-black horse. Use the table to determine what the genotype might be at the C and D loci. What might the genotype of an all-white horse be at the E locus? Is the W locus epistatic? Why might you not want to breed two all-white horses? To complete this exercise, visit the following website:

http://www.biology.arizona.edu/human_bio/problem_sets/color_blindness/color_blindness.html

Genetic Counseling
Estimated time for completion = 10 minutes

How can the average person deal with the rapidly expanding amount of genetic information available to the public and to health-care providers? Genetic counselors serve as an interface between this information and the public. They are trained in both genetics and counseling and can convey genetic information to individuals in an accurate and objective manner. The linked website describes a case study of a family with a child diagnosed with neurofibromatosis. Briefly discuss some of the issues that a genetic counselor may encounter in counseling this family. To complete this exercise, visit this website:

http://www.cancergenetics.org/nf1.htm

Alcoholism
Estimated time for completion = 10 minutes

Is alcoholism a genetic disease? After reading the paper on "The Genetics of Alcoholism," you should be able to answer the following questions. What methods are used to estimate the genetic contribution to alcoholic behavior in humans? Is the evidence of a genetic contribution similar between the different types of studies?

Does the inherited component of alcoholism behave like a simple Mendelian locus or as a quantitative trait? Are any known genes linked to alcoholic behavior? To complete this exercise, visit the following website:

http://silk.nih.gov/silk/niaaa1/publication/aa18.htm

Translation
Estimated time for completion = 5 minutes

What are the steps in protein synthesis? As with DNA transcription, the process requires three steps. The translational machinery must initiate translation, elongate the polypeptide, and terminate the process. These stages of translation require the coordination of RNA and many protein molecules. The website provides an overview of this process and illustrates the dynamics with a short animation. After viewing the text and animation, describe the physical relationship between the tRNA, mRNA, and the A and P sites of the ribosome. Discuss the role of the endoplasmic reticulum in translation. To complete this exercise, visit this website:

http://www.blc.arizona.edu/INTERACTIVE/DNA3/proteins.html

Information
Estimated time for completion = 5 minutes

How is genetic information transferred in a cell? DNA replication, transcription, and translation are the events determining flow of genetic information. While each process is distinct in many aspects, there are similarities in the pattern of information processing. The examination of many cellular processes suggests that a general evolutionary strategy has been to repeat successful strategies in new contexts. In this exercise, you will view short animations of DA transcription and protein translation. After watching these side by side, list as many common features of these processes as you can. To complete this exercise, visit:

http://www.pbs.org/wgbh/aso/tryit/dna/

Lactose Operon
Estimated time for completion = 20 minutes

How does a cell respond to changes in environmental conditions? One of the best examples is the description of the lactose operon by Jacob, Monod, and Wollman. Test your understanding of *lac* operon regulation with a series of interactive questions at the linked website. Feedback will indicate whether your answers are correct, and tutorial information is provided to clarify your understanding. Construct a chart listing the various genotypes and conditions (with and without lactose) and the resulting effect. To complete this exercise, visit this website:

http://www.biology.arizona.edu/molecular_bio/problem_sets/mol_genetics_of_prokaryotes/Prokaryotes.html

Polymerase Chain Reaction (PCR)
Estimated time for completion = 5 minutes

PCR has radically changed the field of molecular genetics. The ability to amplify DNA quickly without a cellular host has dramatically increased the pace of molecular genetics. In this exercise, you will view a short animation of the polymerase chain reaction (PCR). After viewing the animation, list the different-colored molecules and describe what each colored molecule represents. Indicate how many of each type of colored molecule are present after the three rounds of PCR shown, and how many you predict would be present after five rounds of PCR. To complete this exercise, visit:

http://wsrv.clas.virginia.edu/~rjh9u/pcranim.html

DNA Testing
Estimated time for completion = 20 minutes

How is DNA testing used in criminal or paternity cases? The nucleotide sequence of specific alleles provides a unique identifier for each person. Similarly, because a child inherits half of each parent's genetic information, this sequence can be used to determine if two individuals are related. Test your understanding of DNA testing methods with a series of interactive questions at the linked website. Feedback will indicate whether your answers are correct, and tutorial information is provided to clarify your understanding. Discuss whether forensic information is used to prove someone is guilty or to prove someone is innocent. To complete this exercise, visit the following website:

http://www.biology.arizona.edu/human_bio/problem_sets/DNA_forensics_1/DNA_forensics.html

Phylogeny
Estimated time for completion = 15 minutes

How can we determine the pattern of evolutionary relationships among a group of species? The study of phylogenetics has benefited from the increased availability of molecular sequence data. Follow the tutorial on phylogeny reconstruction from molecular sequence data and then answer the following questions. Why do all phylogenetic trees eventually converge on a common ancestor? What is the relationship between mutation and time of divergence? Are all mutations equally useful in estimating phylogenies? What processes might cause different rates of evolution for "essential" vs. "irrelevant" mutations? To complete this exercise, visit this website:

http://aleph0.clarku.edu/~djoyce/java/Phyltree/cover.html

ANATOMY AND PHYSIOLOGY

pH
Estimated time for completion = 5 minutes

Many physiological processes function properly only under a narrow range of pH values. Serious consequences result from an acid-base imbalance in the body. After reading section 3.2 in your text, please visit the website below. Follow the directions there to adjust the concentration of hydrogen ions in solution; note what happens to the pH. This website is maintained by the Anesthesiology Department of Tulane Medical School. After doing the exercise, please explain why pH chemistry is important to anesthesiologists.

http://www.mcl.tulane.edu/departments/anesthesiology/acidbase/playpH.html

Basal Metabolic Rate (BMR)
Estimated time for completion = 5 minutes

What is your personal basal metabolic rate (BMR)? In other words, how much energy does your body require while you are at rest and while you are exercising? To calculate your BMR, please visit the web address below. Read the explanation there, and fill in the information requested on the table. Record your BMR. Now go back to the table and change some values. What happens to the BMR when you change your age? Your weight? Your percentage of heavy or moderate exercise? Prepare a short essay describing how this information applies to your daily routine.

http://www.global-fitness.com/BMR_calc.html

Connective Tissue
Estimated time for completion = 15 minutes

One of the four basic tissue types is connective tissue. Connective tissue is classified in part by the type of matrix— the noncellular material— it contains. The identification of connective tissue is an important skill to master; once you have identified such a tissue, you can surmise its general function. This skill can be difficult, however, without practice. Go to the website below and select connective tissue I and connective tissue II under the Review mode; then click on the Quiz to test your understanding.

http://www.medinfo.ufl.edu/year1/histo/

Bone Density
Estimated time for completion = 10 minutes

The American Society for Bone and Mineral Research published a series of articles about studies of dietary intake and bone density. Please read the articles found at the web addresses below. Reflect on your lifestyle and your knowledge of bone physiology. Do these studies make sense? Will you change your diet or lifestyle as a consequence?

http://www.asbmr.org/99%20Press%20Releases/99release_5.html
http://www.asbmr.org/99%20Press%20Releases/99release_8.html

Bone Quizzes
Estimated time for completion = 10 minutes

Having learned about the skeletal system, you might find it fun to test your understanding of that system. At the first site below you will get a series of bone-related questions. Write your answers down; then click on the Answer button to see how you did. Now go to the next website listed below and try the questions there. Were you able to apply your knowledge of bones to this situation?

http://www.dcn.davis.ca.us/go/explorit/quiz/java_bonequiz.html
http://www.mayohealth.org/mayo/9702/htm/bonequiz/start.htm

Knee Structure
Estimated time for completion = 15 minutes

The knee has a unique structure, combining three articulations in one joint. It carries the weight of the body, yet seems hardly stable enough to function. To examine this joint more fully, please visit the site below. Read the information presented, and study the labeled photographs of a dissected knee. Prepare your own description of the knee joint, including the placement of structures that are typically associated with synovial joints. How can the knees both support your weight and allow for a range of motions?

http://www.hipkneeshoulder.com/kneeop.htm

Spinal Cord Injury
Estimated time for completion = 10 minutes

Reflect on the lives of individuals with a spinal cord injury. Using what you know about the spinal cord, spinal nerves, and their functions, decide how a spinal cord injury would affect you. Visit the website below to see various statistics about spinal cord injuries. How does spinal cord injury change the life expectancy of a person your age? What are the physiological and anatomical bases for the changes? Working alone or in a group, relate the information on this Web page to the information in the text to describe spinal cord function.

http://www.kumc.edu/research/medicine/pharmacology/CAI/webCAI/ua06.htm

Brain Probe
Estimated time for completion = 10 minutes

The frontal lobe of the brain includes the primary motor cortex, which controls skeletal muscle movements. How was the primary motor cortex mapped? Which parts of the frontal lobe control muscles in any one area of the body? To investigate this part of the brain, go to the web address listed below. Then click on Mapping the Motor Cortex: A History. Next, return to the previous page and click on Probe the Brain activity. Follow the directions and map the primary motor cortex, creating a reference for yourself.

http://www.pbs.org/wgbh/aso/tryit/brain/

Allergies
Estimated time for completion = 5 minutes

One of the most common ailments of the immune system is an allergic reaction. What are allergies? To test your knowledge, visit the website below. Answer the eight questions there, and keep track of your score. If you get any incorrect answers, jot down the correct answer and the provided explanation in your notes for further study. What did you learn from this quiz?

http://www.mayohealth.org/mayo/9803/htm/allergy/index.html

Heart Murmurs
Estimated time for completion = 10 minutes

What is a heart murmur? What causes this condition? What does it sound like? To explore these questions, select the keyword **MURMUR** on your Companion Website. After reading the page, click on the musical notes next to each heart murmur type to hear typical murmurs. Can you distinguish the sounds? Using the Web page and the text as references, list the cause of each murmur, and try to describe the change in sound. If you have access to a stethoscope, listen to actual heartbeats. Can you distinguish what you are hearing? To complete this exercise, visit Web Exploration 2 in Chapter 20 of your Companion Website and select the keyword **MURMUR**. [Martini, Ch. 20, p. 687]

GI Tract Quiz
Estimated time for completion = 5 minutes

Although the gastrointestinal tract is very long, it includes relatively few organs. Viewing these organs on paper is not quite the same as seeing them intact in an organism. To test your ability to identify the digestive organs in situ, visit the web address below. Match the organs that are indicated with the proper term, and check your grade. Then take the multiple-choice quiz, using the Test yourself link. How good are you at transferring the information from your text to other images? \

http://library.thinkquest.org/15401/test_diagram_dig.html

Dehydration
Estimated time for completion = 10 minutes

Dehydration is a serious concern for people who exercise in hot climates. It is important to be able to recognize the signs and symptoms of dehydration and to know what actions to take should this condition arise. To learn more about the significance of dehydration and of fluid balance, visit the site below. After reading the article, take the fluid balance test. Determine your personal fluid needs. Prepare a short essay explaining dehydration. Include your fluid balance calculations.

http://riceinfo.rice.edu/~jenky/sports/dehydration.html

Impotence
Estimated time for completion = 5 minutes

Impotence is a serious concern for males as they age. Honest information about this topic is difficult to find other than from physicians. To learn more about impotence, including the various causes and remedies, visit the website below. Read the article, and outline the important information presented in it. Using your notes, prepare an informational brochure that would be suitable for the general public.

http://www.andrology.com/main01.htm

Reproduction Quiz
Estimated time for completion = 10 minutes

To understand the reproductive system, you must learn two anatomies, two physiological cycles, and two similar—yet not identical—hormonal mechanisms. The web address below includes a quiz that covers all aspects of this system. Each question has a tutorial button that provides help in answering the posed question. Test your knowledge of the reproductive system by working through all 12 questions, taking note of those that you miss. Using these questions as an outline, create a reference sheet for your studies.

http://www.biology.arizona.edu/human_bio/problem_sets/Human_Reproduction/01q.html

Human Development Time Line
Estimated time for completion = 10 minutes

Human development from embryo to neonate is a sequential process of change that includes many steps and structures. To help you keep this material in order, review the information at the address below. There you will see a diagram of a fertilized egg and a time line. Identify the structures shown by clicking on the name in the box on the upper right. Information about each structure is given in the box on the lower right. Use the forward arrow at the bottom of the page to view a series of diagrams. Create your own time line, adding information from both this website and your text.

http://www.med.upenn.edu/meded/public/berp/overview/BV_1.html

Surfactant Production
Estimated time for completion = 5 minutes

Premature infants experience a host of problems as a result of their early birth. One such problem is the lack of production of surfactant in their lungs. Please visit the website below to learn about a breakthrough in surfactant production. Prepare an outline of the article's major points. How does surfactant work? Why does this chemical help premature infants?

http://www.eurekalert.org/releases/ucsb-nso082099.html

ECOLOGY AND ENVIRONMENTAL SCIENCE

Biodiversity

Ecologists have long argued about the best ways to track the diversity and integrity— soundness— of ecosystems. This *Web Investigation* allows you to explore some issues we face in developing practical tools for measuring biodiversity.

Investigation 1 (Estimated time for completion = 20 minutes)
How should we measure biodiversity? Most current definitions of the term recognize that biodiversity encompasses the complexity of all life, including not only the great variety of species but also their behavior and interaction. Measurement of biodiversity may therefore require several measures, each with a particular focus and value. To learn about some of these methods, go to the following website:

http://www.nhm.ac.uk/science/projects/worldmap/diversity/index.html

Given the increasing global pressure to conserve biodiversity, what criteria would you use to select appropriate measures? Differentiate between "best" and "practical" measures, as described on the recommended website or a similar resource.

Investigation 2 (Estimated time for completion = 20 minutes)
Who should be able to use areas set aside for biodiversity protection? As nations around the world try to meet their commitments to the 1992 United Nations Convention on Biological Diversity, a growing number are establishing biodiversity preserves that exclude resource extraction, tourism, and recreation. Go to the following website to read about the management of Korup National Park, which encompasses parts of five African countries including Cameroon and Gabon:

http://www.panda.org/forestsummit/korup.html

The proposed conservation plan will include controls on poaching and hunting of "bushmeat"— wildlife species— but it does not offer explicit solutions for indigenous groups who may be required to move out of the park area or seek alternative income sources. Suggest some ways in which the needs of these people can be accommodated without endangering biodiversity in Korup National Park. Who should pay the costs of such programs? Should protection of biodiversity always preclude extractive, recreational, or tourism uses? If not, under what circumstances might conjunctive use be appropriate?

Investigation 3 (Estimated time for completion = 20 minutes)
What obstacles may slow or prevent the protection of biodiversity in ecosystems that cross political borders? Go to

http://www.nhm.ac.uk/science/projects/worldmap/

to view a map of relative global biodiversity values, as determined by the Natural History Museum in London, England. Notice that red is used to shade areas with the highest biodiversity, while blue marks areas with lowest biodiversity. Identify regions that are shaded red or orange— those that may be considered areas most in need of biodiversity conservation. Now, using a text atlas or the online atlas available at

http://plasma.nationalgeographic.com/mapmachine/

identify the nations whose territories are shaded red or orange. For one regional group (Southeast Asia or Western Europe, for example), determine the number of nations in the regional group, and therefore the cultural, economic, or political obstacles to transboundary management of biodiversity that may exist in it.

Resources in *Biology: A Guide to the Natural World*.
Pages 392-416 (Chapter 20) describe the diversity of life and how different forms of life are classified. Chapter 21 introduces plants and plant ecology. The *MediaLab* on pages 478-479 discusses the importance of plant diversity. Chapter 28 introduces the concepts of populations and communities in ecology, discussing the concepts of habitat and niche on page 627. Community interactions are described on pages 625-636.

Biogeochemical Cycles as a Tool for Environmental Management

Biogeochemical cycles provide simple conceptual models that help us understand the sources, pathways, and sinks of natural materials— and the implications of human intervention in those cycles. This *Web Investigation* allows you to explore some of the ways that human actions have affected several biogeochemical cycles, and how those cycles give us clues about appropriate remedial actions.

Investigation 1 (Estimated time for completion = 20 minutes)
How much do your own actions contribute to global warming? Go to

$$\text{http://www.inetport.com/~mlandrus/carboncalc.html}$$

to access a site that allows you to calculate your own carbon budget. Calculate your own personal loadings of carbon dioxide to the atmosphere, in pounds per year, following the instructions on the Web page. If you do not know how to fill in some of the estimates, you can ask your instructor or other students for suggestions, check your home utility bill, or simply try an arbitrary value. (Values for home heating in particular will differ significantly depending on climate.) The calculator also estimates how many trees you would have to plant to remove your personal CO_2 load. Examine this number and think about how difficult or how easy it would be to plant that many trees. How much space would that many trees occupy? Do you think that the number of trees, or the space they would occupy, would create problems if this measure were proposed as a solution to carbon dioxide loadings to the atmosphere? Do you believe that people should be allowed to discharge as much carbon dioxide as they want, provided that they plant enough trees to remove it? Why or why not?

Investigation 2 (Estimated time for completion = 20 minutes)
Do the costs of environmental cleanup exceed the benefits? Resources for the Future (RFF) staff have used the nitrogen and sulfur cycles to assess the direct and indirect benefits of reducing acid rain. To read a summary of their findings, go to

$$\text{http://www.rff.org/disc\_papers/summaries/9731.htm}$$

In the past, acid rain cleanup was targeted mainly at improving the health of aquatic and forest systems. How do the RFF results compare with this traditional wisdom? How do their calculated benefits compared with their calculated costs? How would these findings have been different if RFF had examined a single facility, such as a coal-fired generating station, or a single environmental compartment, such as the atmosphere?

Investigation 3 (Estimated time for completion = 20 minutes)
What is an acceptable level of cottage development on a small lake? Go to

$$\text{http://www.ccn.cs.dal.ca/Science/SWCS/TPMODELS/omeehtml.html\#HD\_NM\_9}$$

to read about a policy proposed by Ontario's Ministry of the Environment in 1990, to restrict the building of cottages (summer homes) on the shores of lakes, depending on the level of eutrophication in each lake. Do the authors of the policy believe that they have enough information about phosphorus cycling and phosphorus chemistry to make firm, accurate predictions about the impacts of phosphorus loadings in every lake? Discuss your view of the scientific evidence that underlies this policy proposal. Do you believe that lakeshore development should be restricted to reduce the potential for eutrophication in lakes? What would be the positive and negative aspects of such a decision for current or would-be cottagers?

Resources in *Biology: A Guide to the Natural World*.
Carbon as an element is described on pages 43–47 (Chapter 3). The box on pages 46–47 contains a description of the processes that form acid rain from sulfur and nitrogen emissions to the atmosphere. In Chapter 21, the importance of phosphorus as a plant nutrient is discussed in the box on pages 424–425. An overview of biogeochemical cycles, including those for carbon, nitrogen, and water, is provided on pages 646–651 (Chapter 29).

Biotechnology in Agriculture:
Weighing Risks against Benefits

Biotechnology may offer tremendous potential for increasing food production, improving food quality, and conserving the environment; it may also create some risks. This *Web Investigation* allows you to explore some of the issues we face using the products of biotechnology in modern agriculture.

Investigation 1 (Estimated time for completion = 20 minutes)
Are the risks and benefits of biotechnology the same all over the world? Go to the following website

http://www.cbi.pku.edu.cn/binas/Library/agenda21/data/ch1.html

to read a United Nations International Development Organization report on the environmentally sound application of biotechnology. (Note that this report has several sections; click on the arrow buttons at the bottom of the page to advance forward and backward in the document.) How do industrialized nations differ from less developed countries in their ability to develop and use the products of biotechnology safely and effectively? Biotechnology could allow industrialized nations to produce exotic food and cosmetic substances that are cornerstones in the economies of some developing countries. Do you think that biotechnology therefore has the potential to increase the economic gap between rich and poor nations? Why or why not?

Investigation 2 (Estimated time for completion = 20 minutes)
How should the products of biotechnology be labeled? Many people have raised concerns about the safety of genetically altered foods. Recently, the agrifood company Pioneer Hi-Bred removed an experimental soybean from their product development stream when it was found that inserting genes into the soybean from a Brazil nut could cause allergic reactions in humans. Some people are also concerned about ethical issues. If, for instance, swine protein-producing genes are transplanted into tomatoes to improve flavor, does that make the tomatoes (and the ketchup and other products made from them) unacceptable foods for religious groups who do not eat pork? A significant proportion of the food sold in U.S. and Canadian grocery stores contains genetically altered material, but little of it is labeled as such. How should such foods be labeled, if at all? Should the consumer bear the cost of such labeling? Go to

http://www.fda.gov/bbs/topics/NEWS/NEW00726.html

to read a recent Food and Drug Administration press release on prerelease testing and labeling of genetically altered foods.

Investigation 3 (Estimated time for completion = 20 minutes)
The Earth's population is steadily increasing, while the area of arable land is not. Farmers are under continual pressure to meet the food needs of our growing population in a fixed land area. Biotechnology offers the opportunity to increase the yield from an important food crop, such as soybeans (i.e., more beans produced per plant), or extend a crop's cold or drought tolerance (so a crop grows well in conditions that would otherwise have been marginal or impossible). Yet commercial application of genetically altered seeds, plants, and animals requires release of those organisms into the environment. Go to

http://www.ucsusa.org/releases/rel.archive.ag.html

to access an archive of news releases from the Union of Concerned Scientists. Many of these articles relate to poor notification of affected parties, and/or unexpected consequences of experimental release of genetically altered organisms. What information, in your view, should be required before a new organism can be released into the environment, even on an experimental basis? What form should advance notice take, and to whom should this notice be given? You may wish to compare your thoughts with the current U.S. requirements of the US Department of Agriculture, and determine whether current rules for testing and notification appear to be adequate. To view these requirements, go to the following website:

http://www.usda.gov/agencies/biotech/laws.html

Resources in *Biology: A Guide to the Natural World*.
Chapter 15 introduces the basic concepts and applications of biotechnology. Pages 286-293 provide an overview of the techniques used in biotechnology, including cloning. Pages 297-298 discuss the application of biotechnology in agriculture. Ethical questions are discussed on pages 298-299.

Certifiably Sustainable?

Does certification that an item is produced through sustainable forest management help consumers make informed choices in buying wood and wood products? This *Web Investigation* allows you to explore some of the issues we face in implementing certification programs.

Investigation 1 (Estimated time for completion = 15 minutes)
Have you ever bought a product labeled by a sustainable forest management program? If so, describe your motives in buying such a product. If not, what factors prevented you from buying the product? If you have never seen a product labeled in this way, discuss the reasons why you think such products may not be widely used or sold, at least in the places where you shop. To review the requirements of that certification program, go to the following website:

http://www.smartwood.org/

Investigation 2 (Estimated time for completion = 30 minutes)
What is meant by "sustainable" forest management? To access a site containing explicit criteria and indicators for the sustainable management of European forests, go to

http://www.iisd.ca/linkages/forestry/indicat.html

These criteria are based on international discussions and are typical of criteria proposed for other forests, including those in the tropics. Imagine you are the person who must implement these criteria— say, someone who is seeking certification of sustainable forest management. Do you think these criteria will be clear and easy for regulatory agencies and forest managers to use? Notice that each criterion has a suggested indicator— something you could measure, to indicate progress toward the desired target. Which of these indicators will be easiest to implement? Which would be a useful basis of comparison with other jurisdictions? Which could you use to determine whether a given forest complied with the criteria?

Investigation 3 (Estimated time for completion = 20 minutes)
Are certification programs always a good thing? To read about the advantages and disadvantages of "green certification," go to

http://willow.ncfes.umn.edu/Steve/grncert.htm

Currently, only about 0.3 percent of the world's forests are certified as sustainably managed. If this percentage increased significantly, what might be the consequences for the forest products industry and the price of consumer goods? Who should audit and enforce green certification programs?

Resources in *Biology: A Guide to the Natural World*, 1st ed.
Pages 457-459 (Chapter 22) describe the structure and function of woody tissue. The box on page 460 covers dendrochronology— the study of tree rings. Pages 635-636 (Chapter 28) describe and show the sequence of primary succession. Forest biome types are described on pages 663-667.

The Ecology of Estuarine Ecosystems

Estuarine ecosystems play a vital yet often ignored role in the health of our planet. This *Web Investigation* allows you to explore some of the issues we face in preserving and protecting these and other habitats.

Investigation 1 (Estimated time for completion = 20 minutes)
How do human activities affect the trophic structure of estuarine systems? Estuaries— the zones where rivers empty into the ocean— are among the most productive ecosystems on Earth, with the most complex food webs. Estuaries are also a concentration point for human-induced damage originating in upstream areas,

resulting in fundamental alteration of downstream habitat, blockage of migratory routes, and increased pollution levels.

Florida's Everglades National Park is one estuarine system that has experienced change because of upstream human activities. Mangrove trees are prominent members of tropical and subtropical estuarine communities. How might removal of the mangrove affect the food web in this ecosystem? What have been the primary human and natural forces shaping the modern Everglades ecosystem? Using what criteria would you consider the Everglades ecosystem to be "restored?" To complete this investigation, go to the following website:

http://www.nps.gov/ever/ed/edmarine.htm

Investigation 2 (Estimated time for completion = 20 minutes)

In your view, would it be acceptable for a regulatory agency to permit the development of structures like dams that have the potential to destroy habitat, provided the agency creates new habitat elsewhere? Some government policies now allow industrial and government operations to destroy habitat as long as an equal or greater amount of new habitat is created to replace it. Justify your position on this issue while acknowledging the biological implications of your decision. In defending your position, address the potential impacts on producers and consumers at different levels of the local food web, the impact of habitat fragmentation on the ecosystem, and the economic consequences for the resolution you've chosen. To complete this investigation, go to

http://www.npwrc.usgs.gov/resource/literatr/ripareco/discuss.htm

Investigation 3 (Estimated time for completion = 30 minutes)

Is it practical to attempt conservation of a species without addressing the larger environment within which it lives? Occasionally, well-intentioned conservation efforts target a particular species without considering that species' habitat, the other species upon which it depends, or the species that depend on it. To learn about a properly developed conservation plan, go to

http://www.darp.noaa.gov/neregion/newbed.htm

After reviewing the conservation plan for the New Bedford Harbor (MA) cleanup, consider the merit and intention of the different action points. Which of the proposed activities are structural (e.g., a new structure or device)? Which are nonstructural (asking people to change the way they behave, for instance in the timing or nature of their actions)? How would each action be likely to affect the overall success of the conservation effort of the estuarine community? If you controlled a foundation with a limited budget to support conservation efforts, which actions would you fund first, and why?

Fire in Protected Ecosystems: Friend or Foe?

The battle has been won: Forest fires are now suppressed throughout North America, saving millions of dollars in damages annually. But what is the cost to ecosystems of removing a natural cycle of disturbance and succession? This *Web Investigation* allows you to explore some challenges of managing fire in protected ecosystems.

Investigation 1 (Estimated time for completion = 20 minutes)

What is the most frequent cause of fire in natural ecosystems? To read about the causes of Florida forest fires between 1981 and 1998, go to the following website:

http://flame.doacs.state.fl.us/General/firestat.html

In 1998, what was the most frequent cause of fire in the State of Florida? What cause of fire creates the greatest damage in terms of area burned? How do these patterns change with the time of year and from year to year? Suggest some possible causes for any trends you observe.

Investigation 2 (Estimated time for completion = 30 minutes)
How do fire, climate, and forest ecology interact? Recent evidence from Siberia provides a 5,000-year perspective on this question. Go to

http://www.uni-freiburg.de/fireglobe/other_rep/research/rus/rus_re_1fir.htm

to learn about the Bor Forest Island Fire Experiment. Do current patterns of fire and forest recovery in that system mimic those of the recent or distant past? If not, what has changed, and why? What clues do these patterns give us for management of the Bor Island Forest in the future?

Investigation 3 (Estimated time for completion = 20 minutes)
How does the scale of a disturbance affect the successional outcome in the ecosystem? To read about forest succession in Australia, go to

http://www.infinitearts.com.au/brain/natural-regen.html

Compile a list of disturbances that can affect natural systems. Identify both natural forces, such as fire and wind (including hurricanes and tornadoes) and human forces such as clear-cutting. In your view, do human influences or natural forces have the greatest potential to create large-scale or frequent disturbance? Explain the reasons for your answer.

Resources in *Biology: A Guide to the Natural World*.
Pages 457-459 (Chapter 22) describe the structure and function of woody tissue. The box on page 460 covers dendrochronology, the study of tree rings. Pages 635-636 (Chapter 28) describe and show the sequence of primary succession. Forest biome types are described on pages 663-667.

Managing Water Resources on a Watershed Basis

The potentially vast range of environmental problems and solutions is one of the biggest challenges for those involved in environmental management. This *Web Investigation* allows you to explore some of the mechanisms used in tackling multifaceted water management issues.

Investigation 1 (Estimated time for completion = 20 minutes)
How big is an appropriate environmental planning area? Go to this website

http://kyw.ctic.purdue.edu/KYW/TipsAndHints/Hints.html

to read the Conservation Technology Information Center's recommendations for watershed management. Think of a river basin or creek in your area. What would be an appropriate planning area for that system, using the guidance provided at this website? If you were to develop an integrated management plan for your watershed, who should be involved? Consider key leaders in your community, people who can provide expertise for the plan, regulatory agencies, universities, public interest groups, the media, and similar groups. What do you think would be the central issues in a watershed plan for your area?

Investigation 2 (Estimated time for completion = 20 minutes)
Who should pay for environmental management that benefits many members of the community? To read about a recent watershed management plan to control nonpoint source (diffuse) pollution for the Lake Mendota watershed in Wisconsin, go to

http://www.dnr.state.wi.us/org/water/wm/nps/plans/mensum/mendota.htm

You will note that this plan was supported by federal, state, and local agencies. Who should pay what share for integrated watershed planning such as this? Who should decide on an appropriate level of planning detail, which will ultimately affect the total costs of the plan?

Investigation 3 (Estimated time for completion = 20 minutes)
How can watershed planning and computer simulation help to anticipate future conditions and prevent problems that may arise in the future? Go to

http://www.magnet.state.ma.us/mdc/WATER.HTM

to read about the Metropolitan District Commission's watershed-management approach for Boston's drinking water supply. Read the details of the Wachusett Reservoir Watershed Protection Plan and the Ware River Watershed Access Plan. Both watersheds will face increasing development pressure over the next 20 years. What is the nature of these changes? What kinds of problems are currently observed or expected in the managed watersheds? How might these changes affect water quality in the watershed, and drinking water supply for the city of Boston? Suggest some reasons why an integrated watershed-wide planning approach may be preferable to planning for a single-use type such as agriculture or forestry.

Resources in *Biology: A Guide to the Natural World,* 1st ed.
The hydrologic cycle is described in Chapter 29 on pages 649–650 and in Figure 29.4. Pages 650–651 discuss human use of, and impact on, water. Global patterns of oceanic and atmospheric circulation, and their relationship to climate and weather (including rainfall) are discussed on pages 659–662. Approaches to environmental restoration are described on pages 670–671 and in the box on those pages.

Measuring Species Change

Biologists regularly track genetic diversity to ensure that a species' gene pool has enough diversity to support a self-sustaining population. This *Web Investigation* allows you to explore some issues we face in measuring and protecting genetic diversity.

Investigation 1 (Estimated time for completion = 20 minutes)
Is it better agricultural practice to plant monocultures or to mix crops? Modern agriculture emphasizes the economic benefits of planting a single strain, but in fact it may be better to intermix different strains of the same species, or different species in the same field. To read the World Resources Institute's position on genetic diversity in agriculture and forestry, go to:

http://www.wri.org/wri/biodiv/gene-div.html

From a farmer's perspective, what are the advantages of planting, cultivating, and harvesting a single crop? What risks might be incurred in mixing different strains of a crop such as corn within a single field? If there is societal benefit in such practices, as suggested by the World Resources Institute, who will reap those benefits? Who will pay the costs?

Investigation 2 (Estimated time for completion = 20 minutes)
Is captive propagation the best means of replacing depleted gene pools? To read about captive propagation techniques for endangered species, go to

http://www.monash.edu.au/pubs/eureka/Eureka_95/freeze.html

To be effective as a source of genetic diversity, captive propagation techniques must encompass a wide range of individuals. Comment on the risks for existing populations in the collection of large numbers of eggs and individuals for captive breeding programs. Suggest at least two ways in which seed banks and frozen embryos could be used by profit seekers for personal gain. In your view, what controls on captive propagation are necessary to avoid such abuses?

Investigation 3 (Estimated time for completion = 20 minutes)
Does the Endangered Species Act protect genetic diversity in threatened and endangered species? Go to
http://www.xmission.com/~gastown/herpmed/bogtur.htm

to read a typical proposal to list a species (in this case, the bog turtle) as "threatened" under the Endangered Species Act. How do the "Available Conservation Measures" listed for this species protect or increase the number of individuals or the genetic diversity of the species, and/or reverse the decline already observed for bog turtle populations?

Resources in *Biology: A Guide to the Natural World*.
All of Unit 3, beginning with Chapter 9 on page 182, deals with genetics. Page 196 describes the role of meiosis in ensuring genetic diversity. Chapter 11 (208-227) describes the foundations of modern genetics, particularly the work of Gregor Mendel. Page 329 (Chapter 17) introduces the concepts of gene pool and species evolution. Genetic diversity is discussed on pages 626-627 (Chapter 28), where it is contrasted with species diversity and geographic (habitat) diversity.

Pests: Kill 'Em or Eat 'Em?

Many people are reevaluating their definitions of *pest* in light of their own value systems and social and economic background. This *Web Investigation* allows you to explore some issues we face in defining and controlling pests in the environment.

Investigation 1 (Estimated time for completion = 15 minutes)
Which do you think makes the more nutritious meal: beef or insects? Food is a central part of every culture. In our own, meat-based society, sources of protein are usually mammals or birds, and insects are viewed as pests. (Imagine ordering a restaurant meal that arrives garnished with a cockroach!) In other parts of the world, however, insects are a common source of protein. Go to

http://gourmetconnection.com/ezine/calorie.shtml

and scroll down the page to the USDA Nutritional Content of Foods Database. Type in the name of a food you enjoy eating, and read about that food's nutritional content. Now go to

http://www.ent.iastate.edu/Misc/insectnutrition.html

to view a comprehensive table of insect nutritional value. Compare the fat and protein content of your preferred food with that of the insects listed in these sources. Which of the two foods is most nutritious in terms of fat and protein? Which would be the better nutritional choice?

Investigation 2 (Estimated time for completion = 15 minutes)
Do you eat insects? If not, why do you think there is a difference between eating a lobster (a sea arthropod) and an insect (a land arthropod)? Go to

http://www.naturenode.com/recipes/recipes_insects.html

to access some recipes that incorporate insects. Insects are a common dietary component in some parts of the world. Why do you think they are not a regular part of most North American and European diets? Have you ever eaten an insect intentionally? If not, why not? Under what conditions might you view insects as an attractive food source?

Investigation 3 (Estimated time for completion = 20 minutes)
What impact does a beautiful lawn have on the environment? Lawn and garden pesticides are now considered one of the main contributors to urban stream and lake pollution in North America. Assume that you are an urban landowner with a front yard area 75 feet wide by 75 feet deep. Go to

http://coopext.cahe.wsu.edu/infopub/eb1744/eb1744.html

to read an article suggesting actions that can improve the health of a garden and reduce the environmental impact of pesticides used on lawns and gardens. Propose a plan for your garden that would reduce or eliminate the use of pesticides, promote healthy plant growth, and reduce the volume of contaminated runoff leaving your lot. Your plan should include a layout of proposed plantings (for example, grass, vegetables, fruit trees, annual flowers) and a list of actions necessary to maintain the garden.

Investigation 4 (Estimated time for completion = 20 minutes)
What ecological principles underlie integrated pest management (IPM)? IPM is now widely used in controlling insect pests. Go to

http://www.nysaes.cornell.edu/ipmnet/IPM.prim.psu2.html#anchor170887

to read a primer on this approach. What do you believe are the main differences between chemical pest control tactics and IPM? Discuss. List three ecological principles that are embodied in the IPM approach. For each, discuss how the principle is applied to control insect pest numbers, impacts, or frequency of outbreaks.

Resources in *Biology: A Guide to the Natural World*.
Pages 392–416 (Chapter 20) describe the diversity of life and how different forms of life are classified. Chapter 21 introduces plants and plant ecology. The *MediaLab* on pages 478–479 discusses the importance of plant diversity. Chapter 28 introduces the concepts of populations and communities in ecology, and discusses the concepts of habitat and niche on page 627. Community interactions are described on pages 625–636.

Tracking Demographic Change

Everyone loves to speculate about the future. But for government agencies, evaluation of future population trends is an essential component of the work they must do to develop public policies— for instance, for education, health care, and social assistance. This *Web Investigation* allows you to explore some of the issues we face in analyzing and forecasting demographic change.

Investigation 1 (Estimated time for completion = 30 minutes)
Is it true that more populous nations have higher birth rates? Go to the following website
http://www.census.gov/ipc/www/idbsum.html
to access U.S. Census Bureau population data for dozens of countries. Create a graph with population in millions along the x-axis (horizontal axis) and fertility rate along the y-axis (vertical axis). On this graph, plot as many nations as time permits. Mark each point with a color to indicate the continent in which the country is located. Use a different color for each continent. Can you identify geographic patterns in the data? For instance, do high fertility rates tend to occur in certain geographic areas? Do high populations tend to occur in certain geographic areas? Are high fertility rates always or usually associated with large populations?

Investigation 2 (Estimated time for completion = 20 minutes)
How do the population characteristics of industrialized nations differ from those of less developed countries? Population pyramids are a graphical means of summarizing the age and sex distribution of human populations. To view population pyramids prepared by the U.S. Census Bureau for many countries, go to this website:

http://www.census.gov/ipc/www/idbpyr.html

Find and click on Belgium on the drop-down menu. Select Summary from the output options, and select medium from the graph size options. (If your computer has trouble processing this exercise, you may wish to try the small option instead.) Then click on Submit Query and inspect the graphs that appear. Repeat this exercise for China and Nigeria. Which of the three countries currently has the largest proportion of people under the age of 15? Which has the largest proportion of people over the age of 70? Discuss the implications for education and health care of the patterns you observed in these present-day graphs. Now repeat your analysis for the 2025 and 2050 planning horizons (the other two graphs provided on your output). In your opinion, what steps should Belgium, China, and Nigeria take to ensure the provision of adequate education and health care in 2025 and in 2050? Propose an action plan for each country.

Investigation 3 (Estimated time for completion = 20 minutes)
For a description of optimistic and pessimistic models of population growth, click on <u>Optimistic and Pessimistic Models</u> at the following website:

http://dieoff.org/page25.htm

What are the major weaknesses of each model? Which model do you find most persuasive? Do you believe that federal and state governments should be concerned about overpopulation and that immediate action is therefore warranted, or do you believe that the risks of overpopulation have been grossly overstated? Give reasons for your answer.

Resources in *Biology: A Guide to the Natural World*.
Page 614 (Chapter 28) defines the term *population*. Population size and dynamics are discussed on pages 615–622. Human populations in particular, including immigration and population change, are examined on pages 622–624. The concept of population pyramids is presented on pages 622–623.